31 DAYS FOR
ADVENT
FOR SMALL GROUP
OR PERSONAL USE

A Strange
Christmas

CWR

Krish Kandiah

Published 2018 by CWR, Waverley Abbey House, Waverley Lane, Farnham, Surrey GU9 8EP, UK. Registered Charity No. 294387. Registered limited company No. 1990308.

For a list of National Distributors, visit www.cwr.org.uk/distributors

Concept development, editing, design and production by CWR

Cover image: AdobeStock

Printed in the UK by Linney

ISBN: 978-1-78259-892-3

Contents

INTRODUCTION

It was 11.45pm on Christmas Eve and I was in church singing a carol. Normally this would be one of the highlights of my year, but that day I felt sick. The last verse came to an end and I made my way over to the pulpit with a blank notebook and nothing useful to say.

As a preacher, Christmas had become my nightmare. So many services in such a short space of time. So many well-known texts. So many expectations of joyful, poignant, punchy sermons. So many visitors. So little time.

I had come down with a severe case of 'familiarity breeds contempt'. I could not see, let alone convey, the significance of the Christmas account, because years of domestication had reduced it to a sentimentalised fairy story.

There was only one thing for it. I had to rediscover Christmas. And in order to do that I deliberately searched out the surprising and subversive, disarming and dynamic truths of the Bible narratives. It was only when I began to realise how strange Christmas is, how revolutionary it is, that I began to recapture the wonder of it all.

This Advent, I want to go on that journey again with you. I want to dig out the strange circumstances that led to the birth of Jesus, and what that means for us and our messy lives. I want to question why people responded in such strange ways, and what that means for the way we worship God. I want to find out why God included such strange people, and make the connection with the tough challenge of a Christmas story that constantly welcomes strangers. And I want to dig deeper into why, according to God's strange wisdom, Christmas is supposed to change everything.

This Advent, let's not be afraid to ask the tough questions: Is God blessing unplanned pregnancies? Why use the forbidden practice of astrology or stellar divination to announce the Saviour's birth? Why make physically unclean shepherds and spiritually unclean Gentiles the most important visitors? Why was there radio silence from God for hundreds of years while the Greeks and then the Romans invaded the Promised Land? Why is Jesus evicted from His home country as a child? What on earth has this got to do with real life today?

Our four sessions will consider the Strange Wait, the Strange Worship, the Strange Welcome and the Strange Wisdom of Christmas. As we struggle to find answers, our journey will take us right through the Bible in 31 daily reflections. It would be especially helpful to get together with like-minded friends (or strangers) once a week to consolidate your thoughts and stretch a little further. There are notes at the back of the book to help guide you in this.

Twenty Christmases after my pivotally underwhelming one, I pray that you may capture the wonder of the season and be utterly overwhelmed… in the best way. I pray that you would read familiar passages and find something fresh and inspiring. I pray that your faith would be challenged, your mind opened, your soul strangely troubled and your heart strangely warmed. I pray that you would relish each moment – to celebrate not only the Christmas traditions, but the Christmas truths in your lives and in your homes.

SESSION ONE

Strange Wait

DAY 1

Strange Plan

Bible Reading

John 1:1–3

'He was with God in the beginning.' (v2)

Daily Focus

It is not unusual for a biographer to start their narrative a few generations before the birth of their subject, so that readers can locate this person's story within the wider context of history. But when John writes a biography of Jesus' life, he starts at the birth of time itself.

I remember one particular primary school football match where the opposing team got a free kick. The boy chosen to take it started his run-up from half a field away. He was so puffed by the time he struck the ball, it barely moved at all. Has John done this here? Has he overestimated the run-up he needs to explain Jesus?

John says that before the universe began, before any big bang, before any elements existed, before any light or anything else existed, there was 'the Word'. Anyone familiar with the opening chapter of the Bible would recognise the allusion. Genesis 1, which also opens with those three words 'In the beginning', refers to the spoken word. When God speaks, things happen. Light, stars, oceans, mountains, hummingbirds, snow leopards and human beings all came from God speaking. When He said 'let there be', then 'there was'.

Just as a monarch speaks and their commands take effect, so God's Word has power. But that power is infinitely greater because His Word makes things appear out of nothing.

God's Word has power. It also has purpose. God's creating words were not His only words. The Bible is packed full of them – words of the prophets, the psalms, the commandments, the history. God speaks because He wants to be known. He wants to show us who He is, what He likes and how we can know Him better. God speaks to communicate with humanity.

They say a picture is worth a thousand words… I wonder how many words a life is worth? According to John, the Word that spoke the universe into being and the Word that communicates God to us, is coming. The world has been waiting for this moment. There is a plan. The creator is about to become a creature and live among us in all our mess.

Christmas is not just a cosy festival to brighten up the winter months. It's not just a marketing win for retailers. It's is not just a cute story to help children sleep better at night. Christmas contains the secret to the universe, to the meaning of life, to everything that exists and ever will exist.

Ponder

Christmas is God's gift of Himself to the world. This Advent, do you hear God's powerful voice whispering to you through the strange and familiar nativity stories? Do you hear the world-creating, life-transforming Word bringing light out of darkness, hope out of tragedy and life from death?

Question to Consider

Re-read John 1:1–3 substituting 'Jesus' for 'the Word'. How does the overall run-up to Christmas affect your own run-up to Christmas?

Closing Prayer

Powerful God, who creates constellations with a word and galaxies with a command, please speak to me this Christmas season – bring light to my heart and life to my soul. Amen.

DAY 2

Strange Promise

Bible Reading

Isaiah 40:3–5

'make straight in the desert a highway for our God... And the glory of the LORD will be revealed' (vv3,5)

Daily Focus

It's hard to wait. As a child, the countdown to Christmas seemed to last forever. Even now I get frustrated waiting for a website to load, or if I get stuck behind a tractor when driving or am left too long in a waiting room.

Imagine waiting *four hundred years* for a promise to be fulfilled! Jesus' coming, planned before the beginning of the world, had been revealed during difficult times as a promise to look forward to. It is a promise of hope, salvation and peace. It is a strange promise of an imminent Messiah who keeps on not showing up.

The book of Isaiah is a book of two halves. The first half contains terrible promises of judgment, because God's people have proven themselves unfair, unfaithful and unfit for worship. Instead of showing a genuine concern for justice and compassion for the vulnerable, they have reduced their 'devotion' to a display of ritualised worship – and God has had enough. They are about to find out what it feels like to be excluded – victims of military conflict, exiled and enslaved in Babylon, evicted from their homes and their privileges. Yet from chapter 40 onwards, there comes the promise of restoration.

It is a strange promise. Strange because even in our modern world of industrial diggers and explosives, it is hard enough to put a tunnel through a mountain or build a bridge across a valley, let alone level the mountain and raise up the valley as the passage states. Strange because this highway in the desert is not for the scattered people to return as they may have hoped. It is a highway for God to come out to them in the wilderness.

Matthew, Mark and Luke all take the time to record this strange promise as part of the Christmas story, and all three see its fulfilment in the arrival of John the Baptist's ministry.

John the Baptist was certainly a voice in the wilderness, and he was certainly calling for God's people to prepare for His coming. But John was not into landscape remodelling or terraforming. John called people to transform the landscape of their hearts and lives in preparation for the arrival of the Lord. This change through repentance, renewal and readying was – and still is – something that cannot wait. Jesus is coming!

Ponder

John was a big deal. We are told that 'all the people of Jerusalem went out to him' (Mark 1:5) but John understood that he was not the main event: the Lord was coming. But even the arrival of Jesus does not (at first) fully capture the language of Isaiah. Perhaps this strange promise holds even more yet to come. What if the time is right for God to come back and transform the whole earth from the mess that it is in?

Question to Consider

Think about the transformations your home is going through this week in preparation for Christmas. What transformations does your heart need in preparation for God's coming again?

Closing Prayer

Lord Jesus, prepare the way for God in our lives. Help us to long for the day when every valley will be raised and every mountain levelled as You come to the rescue of Your people. Amen.

DAY 3

Strange Peril

Bible Reading

Malachi 4:4–6

'I will send the prophet Elijah to you before that great and dreadful day of the Lord comes.' (v5)

Daily Focus

I love Christmas, but sometimes the preparations fill me with dread. Will everyone like my presents? Will my sons join us on Christmas Day? What if my relatives argue again? Can I even afford Christmas this year?

Christmas dread seems unseasonal. It is supposed to be a time of great celebration and joy. If, like me, your Christmas is seasoned with anxiety, then we are in good company because there is the same Advent tension in the Bible.

The last book in our Old Testament before the Christmas story contains Malachi's prophecy, which ends on a cliff-hanger. Written hundreds of years before Jesus' birth, it challenges Israel's half-hearted worship, which does nothing about the needs of the widow, orphan or refugee (Mal. 3:5). It ends by asking God's people to look back and remember Moses' laws. And it looks forward to when God will once again send the great prophet Elijah, bringing either reconciliation or destruction.

The Bible is not suggesting Elijah's reincarnation. But nevertheless, there is a lot riding on Elijah's return. If he fails and there is no intergenerational revival, then the future holds only destruction and judgment.

That's how our Old Testament closes – with a note of mystery and foreboding. Then there follows 400 years of radio silence from God. No prophets, no prophecies, no angels, no miracles, no more books of the Bible.Also no destruction, no judgment.

Four centuries later, the silence is broken by an angel appearing to an old priest. This priest and his wife, who have suffered with infertility their whole lives, are about to become parents. Their child 'will go on before the Lord, in the spirit and power of Elijah, to turn the hearts of the fathers to their children and the disobedient to the wisdom of the righteous – to make ready a people prepared for the Lord' (Luke 1:17).

Not reincarnation – a re-connection. The boy – John the Baptist – will continue the mission of Elijah, preparing people for Jesus' coming. After a long wait, the promise will be fulfilled.

But what about the dark side of the promise – the destruction – will that too be fulfilled? The next time Elijah and Moses are mentioned is just before Jesus starts His final journey to the cross. They appear to Him up a mountain and encourage Jesus to be faithful unto death, so that everyone who trusts in Him can be saved from the coming destruction and judgment (Luke 9:29–31).

There is a right dread about Christmas. In the end it is not about how well Christmas Day goes, or about the right gift choices. Malachi encourages us to put our lives in order.

Ponder

Moses and Elijah represent the whole Old Testament, which is pointing us to Jesus. He alone can rescue us from the peril we are truly in. He alone is the way we can be ready for the future, whatever it may hold.

Questions to Consider

What do you dread most about Christmas? What would Malachi encourage you to be most concerned about?

Closing Prayer

Almighty God, as the great and dreadful day approaches, may we know Christ's faithfulness to save us and bring us peace. Amen.

DAY 4

Strange Power

Bible Reading

Genesis 12:1–3

'I will make you into a great nation, and I will bless you… and all peoples on earth will be blessed through you.' (vv2–3)

Daily Focus

The nativity story is connected with a lot of strange pregnancies. The first of these is Abraham and Sarah's, centuries earlier. It is the story of an unlikely conception, a birth that would happen far away from home, a baby born in a makeshift shelter, a child destined to impact the whole world. This story is more Christmassy than we perhaps realise at first.

Most people looking at the elderly, infertile and nomadic couple Abram and Sarai (as they were called for nearly a century) would have dismissed their usefulness to society, but God sees something more. While others would have written them off as basically 'as good as dead' (Rom. 4:19), with God's power there is life and hope and significance.

In their new, God-given identities, Abraham and Sarah were going to be involved in a chain reaction of blessing: God blessed them with a son – Isaac, whom God blesses years later with an unlikely heir in his second, smooth and slippery offspring – Jacob. This Jacob has many sons who become the tribes of Israel, through whom God wanted light and hope to flow to the rest of the world.

But there are some bumps along the road to the promised blessing. After many trials and tribulations, failing generation after generation, Israel finds itself invaded again, this time suffering under Roman conquest. Then God takes another childless couple and gives them a child, born in a makeshift shelter far from home.

Realising that God is fulfilling His promises, Mary sings, 'He has helped his servant Israel, remembering to be merciful to Abraham and his descendants for ever, just as he promised our ancestors' (Luke 1:54–55).

The apostle Paul makes the link, saying, 'Christ redeemed us... in order that the blessing given to Abraham might come to the Gentiles through Christ Jesus, so that by faith we might receive the promise of the Spirit' (Gal. 3:13–14).

The strange pregnancy in an unlikely couple at the beginning of the Old Testament prefigures the strange pregnancy in an unlikely couple at the beginning of our New Testament. In both cases, the child is the means through which God will bless the nations. Jews and Gentiles, one passing blessing on to the other.

And when that blessing reaches us, we must pass it on to others. Whatever forgiveness, grace and acceptance we know – it is there to be passed on. We too are invited to participate in the strange, ancient global power of grace that began way back with Abraham and Sarah's willingness to trust God.

Ponder

Do you think you are too unlikely or unworthy to be used by God? 'Too old' like Abraham? 'Too young' like Mary? God keeps choosing unlikely people to be agents of His grace. Is He now choosing you?

Questions to Consider

Where will the God of grace call you to go? To whom have you passed on the blessings that you have received from God?

Closing Prayer

God of Grace, we thank You for the blessings that You have lavished on us. Like Abraham, help us to pass on to others the blessings we have received from You. This Christmas season, give us the faith to obey You, wherever and to whomever You send us. Amen.

DAY 5

Strange Prophecy

Bible Reading

Isaiah 42:1,6–7

> *'Here is my servant, whom I uphold, my chosen one in whom I delight; I will put my Spirit on him, and he will bring justice to the nations.' (v1)*

Daily Focus

My least favourite part of a church service is the notices. I zone out while they announce the senior citizen's lunch, request items for the bake sale and flag up the food bank's shortage of long-life milk. But when they mention the free hog roast at the football club – then they have my attention!

The Israelites experienced this several millennia ago, as Isaiah droned on about their impending captivity as punishment for disobeying God's laws and neglecting the poor, the orphans and the widows (Isa. 1:17,23). But there was a light at the end of the dark tunnel: God would send His servant to bring justice. Not just for the Jews, but for the Gentiles too. This servant would reverse the fortunes of Israel. Now that caught their attention!

Perhaps it is understandable that the Jews zoned out of the rest of the prophecy. After all, they were still licking their wounds. And what had the Gentiles ever done for them anyway – except persecute them, desecrate them, destroy their temple and enslave them?

A friend of mine discovered on a recent trip to the Middle East that, there, the measure of Christian hospitality is how you treat your persecutors. He found that very challenging. That is exactly what Isaiah's prophecy endorsed. Providing an authentic welcome to both the persecuted and the persecutors has always been on God's agenda.

When Jesus was born, Simeon recognised this baby as the fulfilment of this very prophecy, albeit centuries later. This led him to sing praises to God, exclaiming that Jesus was the light of revelation to the Gentiles, the salvation of all nations (Luke 2:30–32).

Jesus not only brings light and hope to all the nations – He models what it means to offer hospitality to His enemies. He graced this dark world in all its mess, with His presence. He shared meals with the Pharisees who would later call for His crucifixion. He healed the sick and freed the captives, only to allow Himself to be captured and His own body to be destroyed. The world mocked Him as He died for them.

Ponder

What are we doing while we wait for Jesus' return? Practising the inhospitality of God's people who cared little for the vulnerable, the foreign and the needy? Or practising the hospitality of Jesus, who welcomed all – including His persecutors – giving up His life for them?

Questions to Consider

Why do we so quickly forget that we were once outsiders to God's grace? How can we extend His grace to another today?

Closing Prayer

Pray this prayer, based on Isaiah 42:10.

God of grace, hear us as we sing to the Lord a new song,
Sing His praise to the ends of the earth,
you who are victims or perpetrators of violence
you warzones and all who live in them.
Let those in orphanages, prisons and hospitals raise their voices;
let the settlements where refugees live rejoice.
Let the people of Syria, Sudan and Somalia sing for joy;
let them shout from the ghettoes.
Amen.

DAY 6

Strange Places

Bible Reading

Micah 5:2,4–5

> *'But you, Bethlehem Ephrathah... out of you will come for me one who will be ruler over Israel... And they will live securely, for then his greatness will reach to the ends of the earth.' (vv2,4)*

Daily Focus

It felt completely the wrong place: a beach in Malaysia, sitting on golden sand under blue skies with our bellies full of freshly made curry. Years of associating Christmas with dark, cold days, cosy open fires and hot mulled wine were hard to shake off. That December just did not give us the Christmas vibe we were expecting.

The first Christmas story takes us to some strange places. The Magi go straight to Herod's royal palace in Jerusalem because that's the obvious place for a king to be born. But when Herod gathers his counsellors, they reveal the curious and unorthodox location, marked out for the Messiah's birth by the Old Testament eight centuries before.

Bethlehem was insignificant, a small clan homeland in the back of beyond. Naomi's family fled Bethlehem during a famine (which is ironic, as Bethlehem means 'house of bread') and she only returned when all other hope seemed lost, accompanied by her daughter-in-law, Ruth, who later becomes the unlikely great-grandmother of a shepherd-boy-come-king called David.

David brings food from the 'house of bread' to a warzone to help out his older brothers. He ends up killing a giant, becoming a great king, winning the heart of a nation and more importantly, becoming 'a man after God's own heart' (1 Sam. 13:14).

Centuries later, following invasion after invasion, the nowhere town of Bethlehem again becomes the epicentre of God's story, for God had promised through Micah that despite its insignificance, Bethlehem would be the birthplace of the King who would fulfil all the promises made to David and more. This King would be the true good shepherd for God's people – not just in Israel but in all the earth, laying down His life for His sheep.

Wherever you find yourself this Christmas, whether it is far away from home, or even far away from God: Jesus offers us the gift of hope. He offers us a secure home, based not on our ability but on His greatness and majesty. Micah promises: 'And they will live securely, for then his greatness will reach to the ends of the earth' (v4).

Ponder

Many people struggle with a 'place' at Christmas. And not just the homeless, the lonely or elderly. The feeling of restlessness – of not quite fitting in – affects us all at some point. Whether you have lost much or gained much, we all need to find our place in the family of God that the true King from Bethlehem offers.

Questions to Consider

Where are you with God right now? What needs to change?

Closing Prayer

Reflect on Psalm 91:1–2, probably written by David who knew what it was like to live in the fields around Bethlehem, the caves scattered throughout Israel and the palace in Jerusalem, finding shelter on the job and on the run:

'Whoever dwells in the shelter of the Most High will rest in the shadow of the Almighty. I will say of the Lord, "He is my refuge and my fortress, my God, in whom I trust."' Amen.

DAY 7

Strange Pedigree

Bible Reading

Matthew 1:1–16

'This is the genealogy of Jesus the Messiah the son of David... of Abraham... of Joseph, the husband of Mary, and Mary was the mother of Jesus who is called the Messiah.' (vv1,16)

Daily Focus

Christmas and family are usually synonymous. Family feuds, family food, family fun and family funds are all part of what we have come to expect at this time of the year. Christmas is also when we often realise how strange our families are. The inappropriate joke from the uncle we see once a year. The annual political debate between the in-laws and the outlaws. The unfortunate incidents involving our children's bizarre eating habits.

I once received a book for Christmas called *All Families are Psychotic*. At this festive time of the year I am often reminded of how true that feels. The things we end up stressing or fighting over betray the strange peccadilloes and priorities of our families.

If it's any comfort, Jesus came from a very strange family. Not just His immediate family, but the whole family history. If Jesus was to get an episode of the BBC television programme *Who Do You Think You Are?* it would make fascinating viewing.

To begin with, Jesus is a descendant of Abraham. This means His credentials as a Jew are unimpeachable. This is important, as Jesus fulfils the promise given to Abraham: that through his descendants all nations on earth will be blessed. Jesus fulfils that in ways Abraham could never have dreamt of. Sadly, the Church has too often forgotten Jesus' Abrahamic ancestry and even Christians have displayed anti-Semitism.

But Jesus also has a Gentile heritage. Tamar was a Canaanite, Ruth a Moabite, Rahab was from Jericho, and although Bathsheba was most likely an Israelite, she had married a Hittite. The inclusion of these women in Jesus' genealogy is doubly strange because family lines were normally exclusively male. Many Jews would have been so ashamed of any non-Jewish heritage that they would have omitted any dubious generations. By contrast, Matthew celebrates these women and the nations they represent. Their inclusion is an early warning of an important theme in the Gospels – the promised Messiah has come to save the *whole* world. They demonstrate the irrepressible grace of God.

I wonder if our families can send a similar signal. Instead of hiding the fact that our families are dysfunctional and damaged, could we not celebrate something of God's generous, inclusive grace? Whatever mess we are in, whatever challenges our families present, none of them are too big for God to handle.

Ponder

Think about all the dysfunctional families in the Bible. How many can you identify? There is surely enough material there to fuel any soap opera script. Yet none of that drama thwarts the grace of God from shining through.

Questions to Consider

Who do you think you are? How can you see God's grace at work in your family... despite the difficulties?

Closing Prayer

Father God, from whom all families derive their name – may Your grace shine through our messy families. As we wait for Christmas, give us the patience and faith to believe that You, who brings order out of chaos and turns tragedy intro triumph, can use even our families to bring You praise and glory. Amen.

DAY 8

Strange Pregnancy

Bible Reading

Matthew 1:18–19

'Mary was pledged to be married to Joseph, but before they came together, she was found to be pregnant through the Holy Spirit.' (v18)

Daily Focus

There is a perception that Christians are the kind of people that have it all together: we live picture-book lives with wonderful marriages, beautiful middle-class homes, perfect children, friendly neighbours and amazing social media feeds. That is not only a myth, but also a perversion of the Christian story. Some might even call it heresy. Christianity begins with a poor family, a shamed non-kosher pregnancy and a persecuted people. There are no baby showers, no framed scan pictures, no gender-reveal party cakes. Just a terrible domestic mess.

The Bible reserves sex for marriage; even betrothal, which was a far stronger commitment than our modern engagement, was not seen to be a secure enough relationship for sexual intimacy. So for Mary to be found pregnant before her wedding is a major problem.

Joseph, the husband-to-be, is under no illusions. Despite living 2,000 years ago, people in ancient times were very clear about where babies came from. Mary must have been unfaithful to him. He nevertheless wants to avoid exposing her to public disgrace. Perhaps he still wants to shield her from being stoned to death for adultery. However, he needs to find a way out of the relationship, and because betrothal was a binding commitment, he needs a divorce.

This is surely a strange set of circumstances. We have seen how this moment has been meticulously planned since before the creation of the world (John 1) and foretold over hundreds of years through the prophets. So this is no accident, no happenstance of history. God intended for the most majestic story ever told, the incarnation of His one and only Son, the beginning of the grand narrative of salvation, to involve the domestic mess of a young couple in an occupied nation.

Suspicion, divorce, adultery, a death sentence, shame, disgrace, poverty, exclusion, embarrassment. These harrowing human elements blend into the divinely written Christmas story – and that is exactly what God intended from the beginning of time.

I find this incredibly heartening. God uses the most traumatic of circumstances to bring grace and His presence. God does not merely empathise with the chaos in our lives – He goes further and redeems it. The greatest story ever told, the true story that makes sense of life itself, shows us that God is big enough to handle the strange mess of our lives.

Ponder

God chose unusual and unorthodox circumstances for the birth of Jesus. If you are seeking the safety of normalcy, could you be missing God's plans for your life?

Questions to Consider

Is what you are facing in your life more traumatic than what young Mary and Joseph faced that first Christmas? How can you learn from God as He works in this complex situation?

Closing Prayer

Gracious God, thank You for not shunning the mess of the world, the mess of our families, the mess of society's expectations when You came to earth at Christmas. Give us the eyes to see where we too can be present in the middle of the chaos, so that we may reveal Your love, grace and redemption to those around us. Amen.

SESSION TWO

Strange Worship

DAY 9

Strange Devotion

Bible Reading

Luke 1:46–50

'Mary said: "My soul glorifies the Lord and my spirit rejoices in God my Saviour' (vv46–47)

Daily Focus

Do you ever find yourself singing at odd moments? Do tunes get stuck in your head at strange times? Sometimes when I am running, I find myself singing and my pace getting faster and faster, leaving me struggling to breathe. Sometimes when I am nervous, a worship song comes to mind, with words that I really need to cling to. I vividly remember having a localised operation and consciously humming through gritted teeth.

Mary finds herself singing after receiving the strangest positive pregnancy test the world has ever seen. First an angel tells her that she will become supernaturally pregnant with the Son of God. Then she visits her elderly cousin and is shocked not only to find out that she too is expecting a miracle baby, but that in her presence, and that of the Holy Spirit, Elizabeth's baby jumps for joy.

How does Mary, this ordinary, unwed, pregnant teenager, respond to this strange confirmation of her pregnancy? In lyrics that will challenge humanity for the rest of time: 'I am the Lord's servant. May it be to me according to your word.'

Mary's devotion to God is exemplary. Whatever it cost her – no doubt she was well aware of the social stigma awaiting her; whatever needed doing – she had no idea how Joseph her fiancé would react; wherever she needed to go – she was willing and available to God.

Mary sang despite knowing this baby would not only upend her own social status – but the social order of the whole world. The rich, the proud, the gluttonous and the powerful would be brought down and the poor, the humble and the hungry would be raised up. This is a revolution. Mary is releasing a protest song.

Christmas gives us so many songs to sing. Songs of celebration, of peace, of joy. But how often do we sing Mary's revolution song? Christmas gives us a hope that things are going to be different. Christmas disrupts everything – not just our own souls, but the whole world. It introduces the melody of the world to come, and invites us to sing it out now. Christmas calls us to join the revolution of all things and to model in our lives the strange new order that God is bringing.

Ponder

In some traditions Mary's song is called *The Magnificat*. This is from the first words of the song in Latin, where Mary explains that her soul magnifies or brings glory to God. This is the first sign of revolution in a world where God is mostly ignored. Christmas must mean putting God back in His rightful, magnificent place.

Questions to Consider

How would you have reacted to such a life-changing announcement from God? How does Mary's devotion and understanding of revolution challenge us?

Closing Prayer

Dear Father, we echo Mary's words of praise to You:
You make the last first and the first last.
You scatter the proud and welcome the lowly.
You bring down rulers and lift up the humble.
You send away the rich and fill up the hungry.
Help us to model this revolutionary hospitality, grace and worship
in our lives and on our lips this Christmas. Amen.

DAY 10

Strange Tenderness

Bible Reading

Luke 1:76–79

'And you, my child, will be called a prophet of the Most High; for you will go on before the Lord to prepare the way for him' (v76)

Daily Focus

A recent study has shown that a person speaks an average of 15,669 words a day. I am sure I must double that as I am a recovering extrovert. When I am excited – I need to talk. When I am worried – I need to talk. When I am in crisis – I need to talk. I can honestly say I do not know what it is like to be lost for words.

I would not have coped with Zechariah's circumstances in the Christmas story, struck dumb on the happiest day of his life. It all started when he was going about his usual work, and then an angel turns up and not only scares the living daylights out of him, but makes a shocking revelation that despite his old age and decades of infertility, he is to be a father. That doesn't leave him lost for words – in his astonishment he expresses his suspicion and confusion.

His response, 'How can I be sure of this?', does not sound that dissimilar to Mary's response: 'How will this be?' But perhaps there was something in Zechariah's tone that needed dealing with. Gabriel strikes him dumb.

Poor Zechariah has had an angelic visitation delivering the best news of his life and he can't tell anyone about it! It is months before a word will come from his mouth. I would have been going nuts. What a story to share with his wife around the dinner table. What a conversation starter when people began asking questions about this strange pregnancy in their old age. What a wonderful opportunity to praise God and thank Him for His mercy. What a fantastic theological conundrum to debate in the synagogue.

But when Zechariah is finally allowed to speak again, the floodgate is opened, and he bursts into song, like champagne exploding out of a bottle. His words pour out in praise of God's mercy and faithfulness. Then Zechariah tenderly takes his newborn child in his arms and sings a prophecy over him. The words are taken from what the angel said to him. He has understood God's call on his son's life and he affirms it in this song. He has understood the commitment involved in parenting a gift from God and his song displays that too.

Most importantly, Zechariah recognises that his son John will prepare the way for the Messiah to make manifest the strange tenderness of God. Just as the rising sun banishes the cold and dark of night, so the coming of the Son of God will bring the warmth of God's love and the light of God's truth to all who live in the darkness of ignorance and under the shadow of death.

Ponder

Zechariah's period of being struck dumb and then being miraculously healed becomes a prophetic visual aid of God's tender mercy and power in creating a fresh start. This will be John's message, and ultimately Jesus' mission to the world.

Questions to Consider

Why do you think Zechariah was 'muted'? What do his words reveal about his months of silence? What words have you spoken today and what effect have they had?

Closing Prayer

Merciful God, we praise You for Your tenderness. We thank You for Your kindness in sending light, warmth, hope and truth into our lives. Amen.

DAY 11

Strange Providence

Bible Reading

Luke 1:24–25

'The Lord has done this for me' (v25)

Daily Focus

When I moved into a shared house after living on my own for a while, I suddenly realised how selfish I had become. Why should *I* be the one to empty the bins? How dare my neighbour drown out *my* music with his pop drivel? And why shouldn't I take my time in the shower if *I* wanted to?

I often wonder if Elizabeth was a bit like that. At first glance her song sounds selfish. She has been living in seclusion for five months and all she seems to think about is herself. The baby growing inside her is for *her* benefit – the Lord has done this *for me* she says. He has taken away *my* disgrace. She does not talk about the fact that the child the Lord has entrusted her with will bless the whole world.

Granted, being elderly and childless in ancient times was not only painful but also a recipe for vulnerability. Although her husband was a priest, and there was some onus on the temple to provide for their needs, the lack of children would still have been felt particularly keenly. There would have been a feeling of shame and a social stigma that came with her infertility.

But there is a part of me that wants to challenge the lyrics of her song of praise. Did she not understand that her identity was found in what God said about her, that she was fearfully and wonderfully made in His image? Did she not trust that despite the pain of childlessness, God's grace was sufficient for her? Perhaps she did know these things and was content, yet still felt the sting of others' opinions. Either way, the result is a raw and awkward prayer of thanks.

The problem in reading about Elizabeth's Christmas song, and indeed the answered prayers of Hannah and Sarah in the Bible, is that it is easy to get the impression that if God does not provide us with children (or our heart's greatest desire) then His favour is not on us. But the Bible does not support this idea of conditionality on the grace and favour of God. We need to remember that His unlimited and unconditional favour is towards all of us – He has given His only Son for us. He blesses us with salvation, inclusion into His family and so much more.

Nevertheless, the Bible includes this short song of praise from Elizabeth's lips and what encourages me is its honesty. Like the psalms and like the prayer Jesus offered in the garden of Gethsemane, God accepts prayers that are genuine, human, emotional. Elizabeth's mixed motives, her limited world-view that threatened her 'self-view' – these do not prevent her from bringing her praise to God. Although our praise may betray our failings, God wants our worship anyway.

Ponder

A true sense of identity can only come from God. Whatever else we may look to for purpose or meaning will ultimately let us down. Yet even when we are tempted to look outside of God for our sense of worth, we are still invited to bring our praise and petitions to Him.

Question to Consider

What is it that you are most tempted to find your identity through, apart from God?

Closing Prayer

Lord God, accept our praise, even though we are often distracted by our disappointments and our distress. Lord God, accept our praise, even though we are often short-sighted and self-centred. Lord God, to You alone be all the glory. Amen.

DAY 12

Strange Joy

Bible Reading

Luke 2:8–14

'Do not be afraid. I bring you good news that will cause great joy for all the people.' (v10)

Daily Focus

As tourists in London, we were once walking from the London Eye to the Imperial War Museum. We took a shortcut and found ourselves in an underpass that tourists are not supposed to see. Excited to see the tanks, my six-year-old son was running ahead. Suddenly, inexplicably, he stopped. Gently he laid his hand on the shoulder of a homeless man who was sleeping. Before I could catch up and intervene, the man woke up. He smiled at my son in surprise and the two shared a moment of strange connection. My son has special needs and usually avoids human interaction. I assume the homeless man had not experienced a tender touch for many years. Two worlds briefly collided. There was a moment of peace and joy that transformed that graffiti-stained, urine-reeking tunnel into a place where I glimpsed God's love. Maybe you have experienced the profound presence of God in a similar way. God does not only meet us in our churches or on our retreats. Sometimes He meets us in the strangest times and places.

At the climax of the Christmas story, God turns up in the form of a baby, born to a homeless couple sheltering in an animal stall. Of all the places to pick, this feels like one of the most undignified. This is not the welcome deserving of a King. Then, to make sure we don't miss the point, God turns up to rough-sleeping shepherds in the middle of the night in the form of an angelic choir.

Unfortunately we often sanitise the encounter. In our art, the shepherds are turned into Renaissance figures with flowing robes, immaculate complexions and coiffed hair. The angel's song has become high-brow classical chamber music, with words in Latin.

This is not an accurate reflection of that first Christmas night. Two worlds are colliding. Heaven is invading earth. The magnificent, transcendent display of the angel's song is not an exclusive performance for royalty at Herod's palace. It is not an invitation-only event at the temple for the clergy of the day. The angel's target audience is physically dirty and socially suspect shepherds, men whose nomadic work meant they were often treated with suspicion and derision.

This song gives us a glimpse of God's strange love that accepts the most unexpected of people; a glimpse of peace and joy in the most unlikely of times and places.

Ponder

Does this story remind us of another? Another field in Bethlehem? Another child who would be king? Another shepherd, rejected by men but handpicked by God? God looked not at David's outward appearance but at his heart. This principle is repeated again in Bethlehem's fields, where those usually overlooked or ignored are fetched by angels to witness the birth of the Saviour.

Questions to Consider

When you look at yourself or at other people around you, do you see what God sees? Do you welcome those who God welcomes?

Closing Prayer

We join with the heavenly host from today's reading as we declare:

Glory to God in the highest heaven,
and on earth peace to those on whom His favour rests.
Amen.

DAY 13

Strange Hope

Bible Reading

Isaiah 9:6–7

'For to us a child is born... And he will be called Wonderful Counsellor, Mighty God, Everlasting Father, Prince of Peace.' (v6)

Daily Focus

A picture of three pairs of skis. A small piece of bread in the oven. A child holding a sign saying 'Every Superhero needs a sidekick'. A man collapsed on the floor holding a pregnancy test. People choose the funniest ways to announce they are expecting a baby. Gone are the days when a phone-around with close family and friends was enough. Now, thanks to social media, a whole new wave of creativity has been unleashed. Scanning through pictures of birth announcements, what you catch is a sense of joy and excitement. New parents want the whole world to know that someone is coming into their lives. The unborn child is cherished and longed for – way before the actual birth.

God does not reveal the arrival of Jesus a presumptuous nine months early, but a crazy 700 years early through a birth announcement in Isaiah. Times were tough then. Isaiah had a lot of bad news to pass on. God's people would lose their homes, their freedom and their security. But God did not want them to lose their hope. In the middle of a stream of doom and judgment, God posts His good news.

Then comes a list of strange names. I cannot imagine anybody's shortlist of baby names these days including those that mean 'Father' or 'Prime Minister'. But this was no ordinary baby.

This child will first of all be born to rule with justice. What good news to people suffering under the despotic dictator Nebuchadnezzar, who destroyed the temple and expelled the Jews. This boy will be the Wonderful Counsellor. What good news to people who are in dire straits because of their own bad decisions. This tiny baby will be Mighty God. What good news to people who have seen the consequences of a godless ruler. This son will be an Everlasting Father. What good news to people who need nurturing with wisdom and grace. This child will be the Prince of Peace. What good news to people living in a world under constant threat of aggression and war.

Even in the middle of a world in chaos, God brings the good news of hope. Christmas reminds us of a child that came 2,000 years ago, and will come again soon to fulfil those promises to a world still in chaos. He will bring justice, wisdom, nurture, and peace.

Ponder

UNICEF estimates that each day around 353,000 babies are born around the world. Many of those babies are cherished and loved, but sadly many are not. Too many will experience abuse or neglect. Too many will grow up in poverty, facing hunger and injustice. It was for every one of those children that Jesus, the Everlasting Father and Prince of Peace, was sent into the world.

Question to Consider

Which name of Jesus do you find most inspiring and why?

Closing Prayer

Lord Jesus, our Wonderful Counsellor, our Mighty God, our Everlasting Father, our Prince of Peace – help me to follow in Your ways. May I bring wise counsel to those who need advice. May I bring Your fatherly care to those who need compassion. May I bring Your peace to everyone I meet today. Amen.

DAY 14

Strange Comfort

Bible Reading

Luke 2:25–32

'Sovereign Lord... you may now dismiss your servant in peace. For my eyes have seen your salvation' (vv29–30)

Daily Focus

An Australian nurse who spent years caring for patients at the end of their lives wrote a book called *The Top Five Regrets of the Dying*. In it she reveals the clarity of vision many people gain in their final days. Most of them said something along these lines: 'I wish I'd... lived true to myself, not others' expectations; had the courage to express my feelings; stayed in touch with friends; not worked so hard; let myself be happier.'

The Christmas story includes a song from a man ready to die. But it's the song of a man full of praise, not regret; full of thanks, not grief.

Simeon, we are told, had lived a good, upright life. But it had not been without difficulty. He grieved over the state of his country, and longed for the consolation and peace that the prophets had foretold. He clung onto the promise given to him by the Holy Spirit that he would see the Messiah in his lifetime. And so it happened that he was in the right place at the right time on the right day, just as a couple too poor to afford the normal purification sacrifice presented eight-day-old Jesus in the temple. Immediately Simeon recognised this baby as 'the One', the promised Messiah he had been waiting his whole life to see.

This divine appointment led Simeon to burst into song. Jesus was everything he had hoped for and more. Simeon sings of Him as the Saviour not just of his beloved country Israel, but of the whole world. He sings not only because he has found comfort in life, but because he has found comfort in death.

The Romans were still in power, ruling with brutality and injustice. But Simeon had confidence that everything was about to change. Simeon did not need to see the change himself. He did not even need to feel part of that change process.

As an activist, I see so many things in the world that need fixing. I cannot imagine there not being a need to fight pain, suffering and injustice this side of heaven. What I learn from God's servant Simeon is the confidence that ultimately Jesus will accomplish His mission and bring hope and peace to the world – and it is our privilege to play whatever part God chooses for us in His great plan.

Ponder

Simeon does not beg God for more time to achieve greater things, to be true to himself or to find happiness. Just knowing that Jesus is on the scene means he approaches death not with regret, but with hope.

Question to Consider

What would it take for you to be able to say to God, 'Now dismiss Your servant in peace'?

Closing Prayer

Sovereign Lord, we have seen Your salvation more clearly than Simeon. We know not only Your birth but Your life, miracles, teaching, death, resurrection, ascension and ongoing redemption of this world. Help us to bring comfort to all, to live in hope and to die in peace. Amen.

DAY 15

Strange Maturity

Bible Reading

Luke 2:36–40

'She never left the temple but worshipped night and day, fasting and praying.' (v37)

Daily Focus

'Better to have loved and lost than never to have loved at all.' Considered by many to be one of the finest poems of the nineteenth century, *In Memoriam* was Alfred Lord Tennyson's expression of grief over the loss of a close friend, and it is said that Queen Victoria found solace in its words after the death of her beloved Prince Albert. Maybe you have experienced a great loss in your life, and as Christmas approaches you feel that loss most keenly. As the family gathers around the Christmas table, you miss the one who is no longer there. Sometimes Christmas can feel like the cruellest time of the year.

Maybe that is why the Christmas story of Anna is so precious. We know little about her, except that she has loved and lost. We know she is from an ancient lost tribe of Israel and that she is a widow and well on in years (even by today's standards), and she also carries the title 'prophet'. But the detail Luke focuses on is that in response to grief, she dedicates the rest of her life to God. Anna's bereavement is life-defining – but in place of bitterness, she chooses devotion.

In the ancient world, widows were especially vulnerable and in many circles regarded as socially irrelevant and politically invisible. But throughout Scripture, God shows special regard for the widow, the vulnerable and the outcast. Luke's Gospel is full of unusual characters that God wants us to pay attention to, and Anna is one of them.

Anna's calling had always involved communication between God and people and her response to Jesus being presented in the temple demonstrates this. She thanks God, and wants everyone to know the hope that this child brings.

Anna, whose name means grace, is not only defined by the life she chooses after she has lost, but also by what she gains: the privilege of being one of the first people to recognise Jesus, and the responsibility of being one of the first to evangelise. Her great grief is turned into great grace.

Whether we are old or young, male or female, single or married, rejoicing or grieving, we have a gift from God to enjoy and to share this Christmas. I find great challenge and great comfort in Anna's story. I am challenged to not let the losses in my life define me, but instead to delight in God's purposes as I put my faith in His promise and my confidence in His character. I am comforted by God's care and tenderness towards a vulnerable widow as He proves once again that He is 'a father to the fatherless, a defender of widows' (Psa. 68:5).

Ponder

We began our reading with Anna's maturity of grace and wisdom and ended with Jesus' maturity in grace and wisdom. This strange maturity is a gift from God.

Question to Consider

How can we bring the hope of Jesus to those who find Christmas a particularly hard time of grief and loss?

Closing Prayer

Anna knew the great comfort that Jesus would one day speak of in Matthew 5:4,6 – and so can we.

Blessed are those who mourn, for they will be comforted.
Blessed are those who hunger and thirst for righteousness, for they will be filled. Amen.

DAY 16

Strange Humility

Bible Reading

Philippians 2:5–11

'In your relationships with one another, have the same mindset as Christ Jesus' (v5)

Daily Focus

I love Christmas songs. From the first day of December, my playlist of 150 festive songs is ready and on repeat. There are classic tracks that remind me of childhood Christmases, others that I know my kids will like and there are a few songs on there that I think I might be one of the only people on the planet to enjoy. My playlist does not contain those painfully inane songs that are on a never-ending loop in every supermarket and department store in the run-up to Christmas. I often feel sorry for beleaguered shopworkers who must feel like they are being psychologically tortured by mindnumbing musical banality for the entire season. I wish I could loan them my catalogue of great Christmas tunes.

One little-known Christmas song, perhaps the first ever Christmas carol, is contained in Paul's letter to the Philippians. This song has no mention of snow, bells, trees or reindeer. Paul's carol is truly inspirational, with a wonderfully poetic description of Jesus' incarnation and mission, a lyrical feast on the theology of Christmas.

The first part describes Jesus' descent. Like a rescue diver leaving the safety of a helicopter, diving into the sea to pull someone to safety, so Jesus jumps from the glory of heaven to descend lower and lower through humiliation upon humiliation. Not only did He agree to save us, but He became human. Not just human, but a convicted criminal. Not just a lowlife, but a low death. Not just death, but the most painful and degrading death – by crucifixion.

We see something of this descent at Christmas. Jesus leaves His throne of glory to come to earth – to Israel under Roman occupation; to a Jewish family – a poor family with unmarried parents. He is born in a small town, and as if that were not humiliating enough, He is laid in an animal feeding trough.

This Christmas hymn does not just point out the descent of Jesus: the second part gives us a sneak preview of what lies ahead. As foreign travellers and shepherds knelt in worship before the baby boy, so one day every knee will bow when God exults Jesus to the highest place.

Too many of our Christmas songs sentimentalise Christmas. There are songs about snowmen, mistletoe, chestnuts and fireplaces. Perhaps if we listen again to Paul's epic Christmas carol, we will break out from the mindnumbing monotony of jingles and elevator 'muzak' and hear instead the majestic sounds of the great Christmas symphony of God's incredible plan to rescue, redeem and restore the whole of creation.

Ponder

Paul's song is contained in a letter written to help a church facing some major relational problems. I find that encouraging as the only churches I have been to that don't have any obvious relational problems are the ones that are so big that at first glance no one seems to know anyone else! Paul pleads with his readers to sort out the relationships, using Jesus' humility as our model.

Question to Consider

How does Christ's attitude – of putting the needs of others and obedience to God first – challenge your attitudes this Christmas?

Closing Prayer

Dear God, help us in humility to value others above ourselves, not looking to our own interests but to the interests of others. Amen.

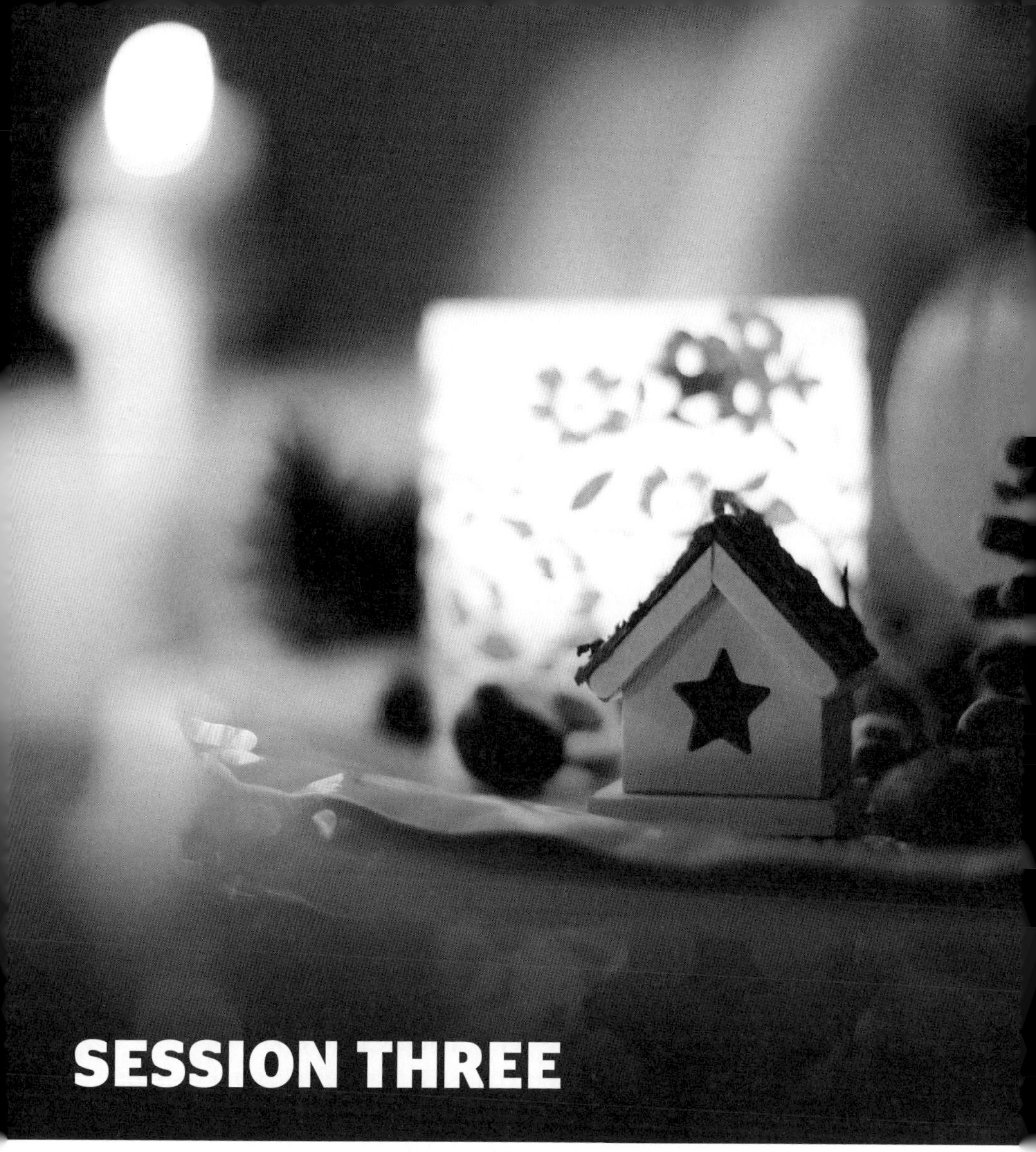

SESSION THREE

Strange Welcome

DAY 17

Strange Arrival

Bible Reading

Luke 2:16–20

'Mary treasured up all these things and pondered them in her heart.' (v19)

Daily Focus

I remember the first time I was invited to my girlfriend's house for Christmas. It was a momentous occasion. It meant I was not just any old boyfriend. After all, it was not just any old meal or any old occasion. Being welcomed to share Christmas meant being welcomed into the family.

That milestone Christmas having gone well, and a wedding later... I remember the time our first child was born. It was a momentous occasion. There was a lot to learn. There was a lot of bonding going on. I wanted to tell the world, but at the same time I was fiercely protective. Only the closest family members were allowed to visit, and with very short time slots.

There was no such privacy available for Mary and Joseph following Jesus' birth. That same night, the first Christmas, God invited some strange people to participate in the intimate family bonding time.

We don't know if they knocked first, if they crept in on tiptoes, or burst in singing the angels' song. The shepherds probably had to explain the celestial choir invitation because Luke, scholars think, gleaned much of his information from speaking to Mary. But what we do know is that these unlikely strangers were welcomed into the makeshift maternity ward to peer at the newborn baby in the manger. They had no right to be there; they were neither blood relatives nor friends. But thanks to the invitation of God and the welcome of Mary and Joseph, they were included in the family that first Christmas.

Then the shepherds went out and told everyone. Their contagious sense of joy and good news PR campaign probably provoked a steady stream of unexpected visitors over the next few days. I'm not sure how I would have coped. Far away from family, no medical assistance, no room at the inn, with a rough and ready crib made out of a trough and random strangers dropping by on impromptu visits. This isn't how anyone pictures their first child's earliest days.

After all the exertion and drama, you could forgive Mary for getting impatient or short-tempered. But we are told that 'Mary treasured up all these things and pondered them in her heart'. On that first Christmas as the young couple welcomed Jesus into the world, they simultaneously welcomed strangers into their lives and into their hearts.

Who will you invite to share Christmas with you this year? Friends and family only? Or are you willing to receive strangers that God may send your way? Will you let them into your home? Will you let them into your heart?

Ponder

Later, Simeon will warn Mary that because of Jesus 'a sword will pierce your own soul'. We know all too well what lies ahead for this baby born in a manger and this mother storing memories in her heart. To welcome Jesus, to welcome strangers is to welcome suffering too. But by the grace of God, He gives us treasure to draw on in those times.

Question to Consider

Who will you welcome into your home and your life this Christmas?

Closing Prayer

God of the outcast, help me, like Mary, to open my home and heart to strangers. For Your sake. Amen.

DAY 18

Strange Acceptance

Bible Reading

Matthew 1:20–24

'When Joseph woke up, he did what the angel of the Lord had commanded him and took Mary home as his wife.' (v24)

Daily Focus

'I could never love someone with no biological connection to me.' It's one of those things people commonly say when I tell them that half my children are adopted. I bite my tongue not to be rude. Half a second's reflection will show how ridiculous a comment it is. The lack of a genetic connection doesn't stop people falling in love and getting married. Even the huge biological difference between man and dog doesn't preclude canines from being many people's best friends.

The myth that DNA gives you a distinct advantage in loving a child is pervasive. But I can testify the opposite. I love all six of my children with the same love, the same ferocious passion. Despite the stigma and fear, I will always promote fostering and adoption until every child has a loving family. I am particularly passionate about calling the Church to action on this issue because adoption is a vital part of every Christian's story.

Take a look at Joseph, for example. He was an honourable man. He did not want Mary shamed or stoned to death for her apparent infidelity. But God spoke to Joseph in a dream to encourage him to accept Mary as his wife and adopt Jesus as his son. There is no biological link between Joseph and this baby. He is Someone Else's child. Yet God asks Joseph to welcome this child as his own. To love Him like a father would. To love the child's mother like His father would. To bring them home like a father would.

Joseph is told to name the boy Jesus, which means 'God to the rescue'. He is also told to think of Jesus as 'Immanuel – God with us', alluding to Isaiah's ancient prophecy (Isa. 7:14; 8:8). Just imagine the responsibility God is giving Joseph – to care for the little boy as he would care for God Himself.

This is an important theme – not just in Matthew's Gospel but in the whole of Scripture. We are told that when we welcome someone into our homes, we are to serve them as if we are serving God Himself – just like Abraham did (Gen. 18), just like the righteous do routinely (Matt. 25), just like countless others have done (Heb. 13:2).

Joseph adopted Jesus into his earthly family. And because of what Jesus did on the cross, Joseph could be adopted into God's heavenly family. Like Joseph, we too can be part of both stories – knowing that we are adopted by God, and welcoming vulnerable children into our lives, caring for them as though caring for God Himself.

Ponder

The Bible is full of stories of adoption and welcoming the vulnerable. Take a look at my books *God is Stranger* and *Home for Good* for a more thorough exploration of these themes.

Question to Consider

Who is God asking us to accept and include in our family?

Closing Prayer

Pray these words, based on those written by the apostle Paul in Ephesians 1:3–5:

We praise our Almighty God who is Father to us, and to our Lord Jesus Christ, who has blessed us in every way through Jesus, who chose us before the world's creation to be His holy people. He lovingly predestined us for adoption as co-heirs with Christ in accordance with His pleasure and will. All glory and honour goes to You, my Lord and my God! Amen.

DAY 19

Strange Hospitality

Bible Reading

Luke 2:1–7

'She wrapped him in cloths and placed him in a manger, because there was no guest room available for them.' (v7)

Daily Focus

He is in every nativity play. Some say he is the hero of the show. Some say without him Jesus would have had nowhere to be born. Some say he is the perfect role model for how to live in xenophobic days. But like the donkey, the blue dress and the infant's halo, the innkeeper is nowhere to be seen in the biblical account.

We have only circumstantial evidence to infer his (or her – or their) existence. We know it was a long walk (33 hours' trek on today's tarmacked Route 65, according to Google maps) from Nazareth to Bethlehem. We imagine Mary, heavily pregnant, walking slower than average on the dirt track. We imagine Joseph after the challenging journey, frantically hunting for accommodation. We imagine the little town of Bethlehem packed full of returnees complying with Caesar's decree that everyone has to return to their ancestral home for the census. So perhaps it is unsurprising that there are no guest rooms available and so the Bible focuses on the manger. We imagine this belongs to someone who has loaned it, along with the shelter, to the couple. Hence we have deduced the involvement of our innkeeper.

Perhaps the landlord of the property where Jesus was born was rich, with space in his outbuildings. Perhaps the owner was poor, living with his family and animals. Either way, someone invisible and anonymous in the biblical account let in Mary and Joseph – and Jesus. That first Christmas, someone made room for a young couple in need and as a result, unintentionally welcomed the Son of God into the world.

That reminds us of other Bible stories. Abraham welcomed three visitors – one at least turned out to be the Lord. Lot welcomed wandering travellers in the night who turned out to be angels. The disciples on the Emmaus road invited a stranger to stay with them – who turned out to be Jesus. There is a rich theme throughout the pages of the Bible – one which shows us that hospitality to those in need is vital to growing in intimacy with God Himself. In fact, in Jesus' parable of the sheep and the goats, hospitality to the needy is the litmus test of genuine saving faith (Matt. 25:31–46).

Christmas is often the time of year when we are most hospitable – drinks for the neighbours, dinner for our extended family, even a drop-in invitation for friends at church likely to be otherwise alone on Christmas Day.

The invisible, inferred innkeeper challenges us. What about welcoming strangers as well as friends, those in unusual need as well as those in our usual networks? What about making this type of hospitality not just a yuletide gesture, but a year-round habit?

Ponder

Jesus' birth was more than a token gesture. It was an incredible act of hospitality as He sacrificially put aside His own home comforts to welcome sinners into His family for good.

Question to Consider

What will you do if you see someone in need today?

Closing Prayer

Lord of hosts, thank You for making room for us to live in the world You created. Thank You for preparing room for us to live in Your new world. Amen.

DAY 20

Strange Guidance

Bible Reading

Matthew 2:7–11

'they opened their treasures and presented him with gifts of gold, frankincense and myrrh.' (v11)

Daily Focus

I like to blend in when I travel. I wear culturally acceptable clothes. I learn a few words of the language. I carry my camera and maps in an unassuming bag. But sometimes I give myself away. I once joined a bread queue in Russia. When I got to the front and saw how cheap it was, I bought four loaves. Every head turned as I walked home; every tongue tutted. I suddenly saw myself through their eyes – a greedy foreigner stealing their families' precious nourishment.

Heads would have turned when the Magi – travellers from Persia or Asia Minor – arrived in Jerusalem that first Christmas, looking and sounding foreign. Tongues would have tutted too. They were not Jewish. They were unclean.

After following the star, the Magi followed protocol and headed to the palace. Ironically, the king famous for executing members of his own family actually welcomed in the foreigners. Herod knew something about the art of the deal. He had already made a deal with the Romans so he could remain in power. Perhaps he was greedy for another deal with this wealthy delegation. At the very least, he gains intel about a potential threat to his position. Herod's serving of hospitality was just a guise for his self-serving hegemony.

At some point between Jesus' birth and His second birthday, the Magi use their God-given global positioning satellite to guide them to young Jesus' family. My mother taught me never to turn up at someone's house empty-handed, and the Magi had the same hospitality philosophy. They came bearing great but strange gifts of gold, frankincense and myrrh.

Just because there were three gifts does not mean there were three Magi. The three gifts had a far more significant meaning. Gold, then as now, signified royalty. Frankincense, a pungent gum, signalled luxury and priesthood. These two gifts were not strange in themselves; what is peculiar is that they were given to a child living in near-poverty. But turning up with myrrh, associated with death, to welcome a new child is as out of place as bringing a sympathy card to a baby shower or party poppers to a funeral.

Just as the innkeeper could not have guessed how prophetic his welcome was, so perhaps the Magi could not know how prophetic their gifts were to a child born to die.

Ponder

God goes to great lengths to include people from other nations into the Christmas story. Profoundly, these strangers who did not know God followed God's star, met God in Jesus and saw something of God's mission sending a King as a pauper, a small-town Jewish child to be worshipped globally, a baby to die…

Question to Consider

What is the difference between good and bad hospitality?

Closing Prayer

As the familiar Christmas carol *We Three Kings* reflects the prayers of the Magi, we also pray in the middle of our own journey of coming to know the King of kings:

'Star of wonder, star of night
Star with royal beauty bright
Onward leading, still proceeding
Guide us to thy perfect light.'
Amen.

DAY 21

Strange Deception

Bible Reading

Matthew 2:13–16

"'Get up," he said, "take the child and his mother and escape to Egypt. Stay there until I tell you"' (v13)

Daily Focus

The radio broadcast was interrupted by an English voice instructing us to gather urgently at the embassy. We packed some quick essentials into a backpack, stuffed cash into our socks and carefully made our way across town as automatic gunfire went off around us. There was an acute sense of danger – the country we were living in was in turmoil. There was also a great sense of relief – we were being evacuated to safety. And there was a deep sense of grief as we left behind friends and neighbours in a desperate situation.

I imagine Joseph felt this and more. He was responsible not just for his wife, but for his baby too, and they were not fleeing towards home but to a strange country. He may also have felt responsible for the tragedy: the whole reason for the imminent danger to Bethlehem's families was Herod's search-and-destroy mission for Joseph's own baby boy. Joseph didn't hang around. He followed God's direction, leaving that very night to become refugees in Egypt.

I once spoke at a carol service at York Minster. The ancient and astonishingly beautiful building was packed. We were instructed to stand for the formal procession of dignitaries and choristers. But the large group of people walking down the centre of the minster did not look like dignitaries and choristers. They were casually dressed, wrapped up against the elements, carrying suitcases and backpacks. We were supposed to be reminded of the images of displaced people from our television screens as men, women and children escaped tragedy in Syria. And in the middle of this crowd there was a young man, walking with his heavily pregnant wife. It was a powerful visual reminder that at the heart of the Christmas story, we are shown that Jesus was a refugee.

For refugees today, what comfort can be taken from this! Jesus knows something of the uncertainty, fear and shame of being forced out of your home and having to flee for your life. For those of us who have homes we feel safe and secure in, what challenge there is here! We cannot claim to worship the Jesus who was born into such terrible trouble, and not be sympathetic to the plight of the 22 million refugees in the world right now.

Ponder

As this Joseph sought refuge in Egypt, it reminds us of the Old Testament Joseph whose family wanted him dead, but who also escaped to Egypt as a trafficked child instead (Gen. 27). It also fulfils an ancient prophecy that God would call His Son (initially referring to the Israelites) out of Egypt (Hosea 11).

Question to Consider

What can you do this Christmas – practically and symbolically – to empathise with refugees today?

Closing Prayer

We draw comfort for ourselves and compassion for others, from the words of Psalm 9:9–10, written by another king who wandered in exile for many years:

'If I rise on the wings of the dawn,
if I settle on the far side of the sea,
even there your hand will guide me,
your right hand will hold me fast.'
Thank You, Lord. Amen.

DAY 22

Strange Rush

Bible Reading

Mark 1:9–11

'as Jesus was coming up out of the water, he saw heaven being torn open and the Spirit descending on him like a dove.' (v10)

Daily Focus

'Just get to the point already!' Maybe it is because life is busy or because I am getting more impatient as I age, but I find myself shouting at books that take too long to get to the plot, sermons that meander, meetings that seem to have no point or purpose. When I noticed my young daughter fast-forwarding through the credits of a Netflix movie, I knew my activity quest had infected her too.

Perhaps that is why I love the Gospel of Mark. He doesn't mince his words; he jumps straight into the action. He doesn't bother with genealogies, scene-setting or long descriptions. He doesn't even bother telling the Bethlehem nativity story. The first time we meet Jesus in Mark's biography is as a grown man striding out into a river to get baptised.

But don't be misled. This *is* the Christmas story in Mark's Gospel. This is Mark introducing us to Immanuel, God with us. Jesus had no need to be baptised. It symbolised repentance and the washing away of sin; but Jesus had nothing to repent of, no sin to confess. His baptism symbolised the astonishing act of sinless God identifying with sinful humanity: Jesus as one with us.

This is Mark introducing us to the Saviour of the world. Jesus is taking the guilt on our behalf. Imagine a child in the classroom who has refused to join in the collaboration to steal the teacher's wallet. When the teacher asks who is responsible, the innocent child owns up to the crime. This is what is going on when Jesus is baptised. He is saving the world.

This is Mark introducing us to the Son of God. In the other versions of the Christmas story, the angel tells Mary that she will give birth to God's Son. In Mark's Gospel, God Himself announces it as Jesus comes out of the water.

This is Mark introducing us to the Holy Spirit's involvement. In Luke's Gospel, an angel announces this. In Mark's Gospel there is a visual descent of a dove, reminding us also of the creation story when the Spirit of God hovered over the surface of the deep.

Mark launches his visually dynamic, action-packed story of Jesus with this event, thereby telling the Christmas story in a fresh way. Mark is in a hurry to help us understand Jesus. This Christmas, may we be like Mark and make haste to make our Saviour known.

Ponder

Jesus was not ashamed to be baptised, even though He was without sin. Contrast this with our timidity or anxiety when it comes to identifying with people we consider beneath us or dissimilar from us. How can we let Jesus' humility set the tone for our lives?

Question to Consider

How does chapter one of Mark's Gospel teach themes of Strange Waiting and Strange Welcome that we have considered in this study so far?

Closing Prayer

Saviour of the world, help us to be like Mark: to have a sense of urgency in wanting to know You more, and in sharing the incredibly good news of who You are, with the people in our world. Amen.

DAY 23

Strange Rejection

Bible Reading

John 1:9–14

'He came to that which was his own, but his own did not receive him.' (v11)

Daily Focus

I once injured my head, leaving a prominent scar. I was a little self-conscious about it, but carried on regardless. Until I got home, that is. As soon as my infant son saw it, he began to cry. Whenever I approached him, he would run away. Any attempt I made to comfort him only seemed to scare him more. This was a strange and distressing situation for both of us. I loved him, but somehow I repelled him.

When God came to His children with arms open wide in welcome, His children did not reciprocate it; they rejected it.

God's own children, the people of Israel, whom He created supernaturally through the elderly Abraham and Sarah, rejected Him. God had kept His covenant to them through the generations, but they had not been faithful in return. The Jews mocked, oppressed, kidnapped, falsely accused, judged and sentenced Jesus to death. They rejected Him, saving instead the brigand Barabbas.

But John's words ring true at another level too. We are all God's children, created by Him. Jews and Gentiles are collectively implicated in the ultimate act of rejection: the crucifixion. God came with great grace and affection and we turned away from Him. Worse, we bullied, harassed and murdered Him. At the cross, God rejects our rejection, responding with greater affection, unwilling to let any of us perish.

One evening I arrived late home from work and everyone was asleep. I snuck in and went to bed. The next morning I was first up, and as I emerged from the bathroom a pair of eyes in a cot spotted me. He frowned and pretty soon he had woken everyone up with his crying. He was our latest foster child on his first night in our home, and it turned out he was terrified of men.

How could I comfort and love a child who was so scared of me? Over the next few weeks I did everything I could to show him that I was safe. I waited patiently as gradually he got used to me, then he learned to smile at me, then eventually to accept my embrace.

God, our heavenly Father, wants to lavish love on us, but our first reaction tends to be fear and rejection. In His great patience, God waits for us to be ready to respond to His grace and truth.

Ponder

God offers hospitality to a world that is inhospitable to Him. God offers acceptance to those who have rejected Him. His humble, faithful persistence in offering unconditional love to us inspires us to wonder, worship and welcome others.

Questions to Consider

Where have you faced rejection and resistance in your life? What would it mean for you to show the unrelenting love of God in those spheres?

Closing Prayer

As Saint Francis of Assisi is said to have prayed:

'Where there is hatred, let me bring your love,
Where there's despair in life let me bring hope,
Where there is darkness only light,
And where there's sadness ever joy.'
Amen.

DAY 24

Strange Dinner

Bible Reading

Matthew 25:34–36,40

'I was hungry and you gave me something to eat, I was thirsty and you gave me something to drink, I was a stranger and you invited me in' (v35)

Daily Focus

The fact that it is described as a palace already put me out of my comfort zone. I grew up in a working class home and went to a comprehensive school with boys from a similar economic background. But tonight I had polished my shoes and headed to a dinner at the Archbishop of Canterbury's formal residence – the elegant and illustrious Lambeth Palace. En route I had researched the other invited guests so I could make appropriate small talk in the drawing room. It was all going well, until a lady entered whom I didn't recognise. I asked her if she had been to Lambeth Palace before, hoping that like me, she was new to these circles. Her reply: 'Well, I do live here.' It appeared I had forgotten to Google the Archbishop's wife. I spent the rest of the evening trying to hide my embarrassment.

Jesus tells us there is more than embarrassment at stake when it comes to recognising Him: there is a dinner at a palace at stake – one we do not want to miss.

The parable of the sheep and goats is not often preached during the build-up to Christmas. It is too dangerous, too strange for most appetites. But it is the perfect Advent parable as it looks back to Jesus' first coming and looks forward to His second coming.

In this shocking and challenging parable, Jesus tells us to look back – did we recognise Him when He came to us? It is entirely likely that we failed to recognise Him because He came to us in the guise of the hungry and thirsty, the needy and lonely.

If we have provided food, water, company and hospitality to those in need, then we should be encouraged: we have been serving Christ and He will welcome us at His second coming because what we have done for them, we have done for Him. Now, of course the Bible is very clear that God's love is not earned or merited. It is through faith in Jesus' life, death and resurrection that we can be forgiven by God and welcomed into His family. But Jesus' parable forces us to recognise that the test of whether we have received grace and mercy is whether or not we are eager to pass grace and mercy on to others. However, if we have not welcomed the needy, and therefore not welcomed Jesus, then He will not welcome us when He comes again in glory.

The parable reminds us that welcome and hospitality is an essential indicator of saving faith. Jesus tells us this parable not just to protect us from embarrassment, but to protect us for eternity. As He prepares a feast for us, we can prepare a feast for Him, by welcoming the least, the lost, the last and the lonely.

Ponder

Too many Christians live as if care for the poor is an optional extra for the few. Jesus indicates that hospitality is the quintessential Christian virtue and warns us of the consequences of neglecting the needy.

Questions to Consider

Do you feel ready for the return of Christ? On what is your confidence or lack of it based?

Closing Prayer

Dear Lord, help us to see You in every stranger who we meet and serve. Amen.

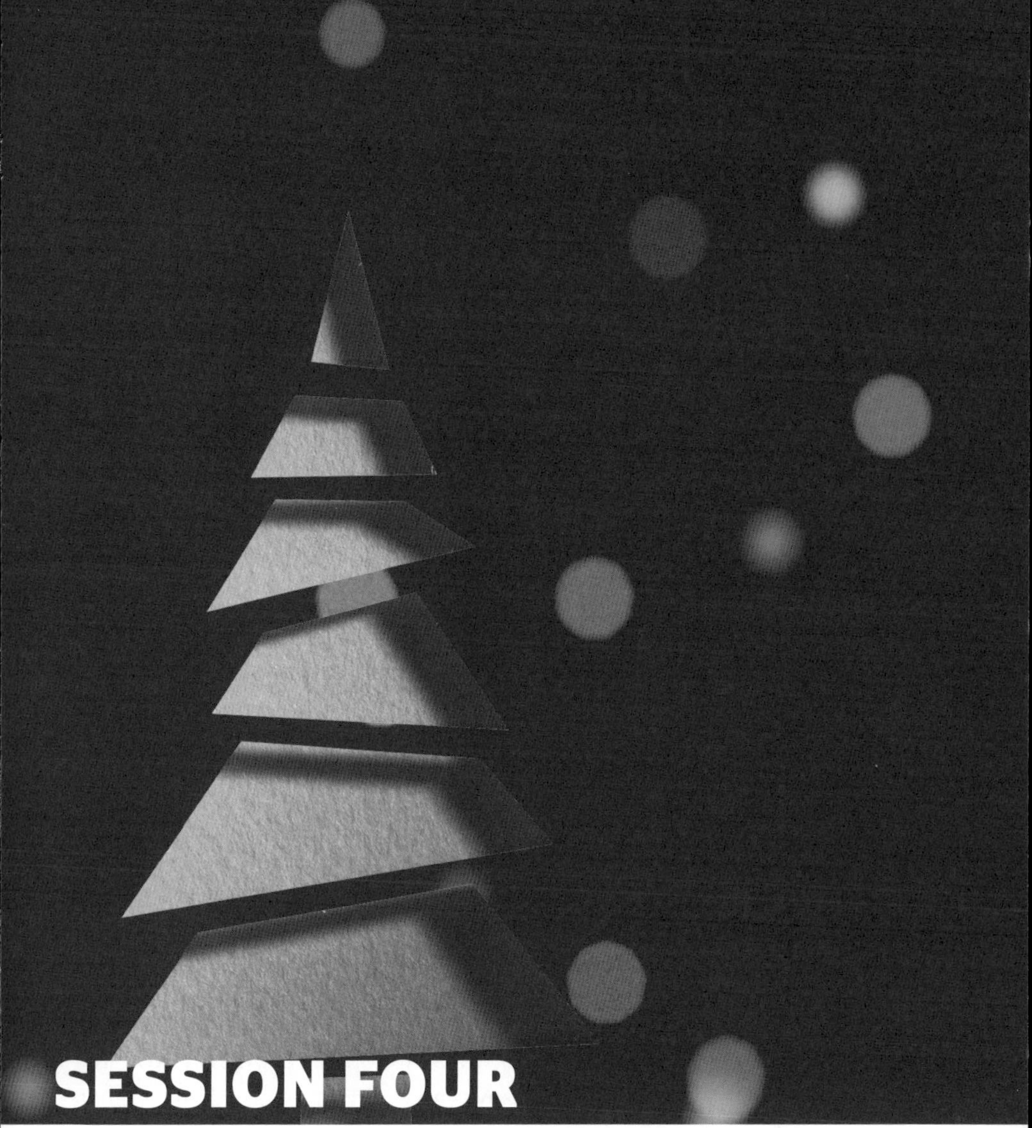

SESSION FOUR

Strange Wisdom

DAY 25

Strange Name

Bible Reading

Matthew 1:20–23

'you are to give him the name Jesus, because he will save his people from their sins... and they will call him Immanuel (which means 'God with us').' (vv21,23)

Daily Focus

Some people buy books or scour the internet when it comes to the task of choosing a name for their child. My wife and I watched films, paying particular attention to the credits at the end. After all, these names signified internationally successful and respected people in the film industry. What more could we want for our child?

Joseph and Mary did not get the job of choosing a name for their child. God provided two names: Jesus and Immanuel. The names were more than just nice-sounding Jewish names. They were more than just a thinly disguised wish of the parents for the child's future direction. They were to be a sign of hope for the world from God Himself.

Jesus was quite a common name, meaning 'Jehovah is salvation', or 'God to the rescue'. In fact it is another version of Joshua, the name given to the Old Testament hero whose victories were clearly won in God's power. At one level, Jesus was an ordinary man with an ordinary name that pointed to an extraordinary God.

Immanuel however, was uncommon. The title appears in three other places in the Bible, all of them in the prophecy of Isaiah, which predicted that the virgin would be with child and He would be called 'Immanuel', which means 'God with us'. Jesus was not just an ordinary man, He was God Himself – with, among and alongside His people.

The names 'Jesus, Immanuel' richly and profoundly signify God in human flesh, the God-Man, the incarnate Son of God. The strange name, given under strange circumstances, raises many questions. How could God become man and still sustain the universe? How could a man be God and yet still potentially sin? How could the omnipresent God confine Himself to one place? How could the omnipotent God become a helpless babe?

We may not fully grasp the implications of Jesus Immanuel, but what we can grasp is exciting and precious. God walks in our shoes. God does not just sympathise with us, but empathises with us. God experiences life as a creature, knowing the limitations and vulnerabilities of a baby. God knows what it is like to be tired, hungry, thirsty, in mourning, in temptation, in pain and dying. God sent Jesus into the world to show us that He can both relate to us and represent us to God.

Ponder

The doctrine of the incarnation is the conviction that God in Christ took on human flesh and yet did not diminish His deity. Jesus was fully God and fully man. This is a great truth we would do well to ponder on.

Question to Consider

How does knowing that Jesus Immanuel is able to empathise with your life encourage you today?

Closing Prayer

Since the 15th century, Christian saints have sung this carol, beckoning our timeless God to 'Come, Lord':

'O come, O come, Immanuel
And ransom captive Israel
That mourns in lonely exile here
Until the Son of God appear,
Rejoice! Rejoice! Immanuel
Shall come to thee, O Israel.'
Amen.

DAY 26

Strange Family

Bible Reading

Galatians 4:4–7

'God sent his Son… to redeem those under the law, that we might receive adoption to sonship.' (vv4–5)

Daily Focus

I have only ever been summoned to court twice. The first time was for an unpaid council tax bill, which had been sent in error. We don't talk about that much. The second was for the adoption of our fourth child. That was a most memorable occasion. As the judge made the final decision, the two-year-old girl in my arms became a Kandiah, a sister to my birth children and a daughter to me and my wife. She could legitimately call me Daddy. And there was no way it could be undone.

Christmas is a time when we celebrate as families. But Christmas also challenges our concept of family. We have already begun to see that adoption is central to Christmas.

In his letter to the Galatians, Paul spells that out in historical, legal and practical terms. He explains why Jesus came into the world at exactly the right time in human history. This was no accident. This was a mission. The first part of the mission was to liberate us – Jesus was born to free us from sin, guilt and punishment. That is worth celebrating by itself! But sometimes we are so busy celebrating that part, we forget there is more good news to come.

The second part of the mission was to adopt us. God releases us from captivity so that we may be part of His family; heirs forever with His Son Jesus; formally recognised as God's child, able to call Him Abba, Father.

Many people think adoption is only for those who can't conceive and birth children, and those for whom IVF has failed. In other words, adoption is a means by which *parents* with a traumatic fertility history find a child or two. But what if adoption is seen as a means by which *children* with a traumatic life history find a parent or two?

This is the Christmas model of adoption. God was not incapable of having children – He had Jesus, the perfect Son. He did not need more children to make His life complete. He was not bored, lonely or lacking anything. God adopted us not because He needed it, but because we needed it. God saw us as we really are: broken, in need and unable to offer Him anything, but still He decided to adopt us into His family, even at the great cost of sending the perfect and only Son He already had, to die in our place.

I meet many children waiting for a family to adopt them. This Christmas, perhaps you or a family you know could consider welcoming a child into your lives through adoption as an overflow of the adopting grace that God has poured into our lives.

Ponder

Adoption is often low down on our list of gifts received from God, but it is arguably the highest privilege that God could possibly give us.

Questions to Consider

What are the many benefits of being adopted into God's family? How can we pass those benefits on?

Closing Prayer

As today's verses remind us of our true identity, we rejoice and pray:

Abba Father,
I am no longer a slave to fear.
I am Your child!
How can I thank You?
Amen.

DAY 27

Strange King

Bible Reading

Mark 10:41–45

'whoever wants to become great among you must be your servant, and whoever wants to be first must be slave of all.' (vv43–44)

Daily Focus

A family I know dreads the serving of the Christmas dinner gravy. That is the inevitable moment the mood changes. Somebody lobs in a critical comment and suddenly it all falls apart. We shouldn't be surprised that families tend to argue at Christmas. With so many people living in unusually close proximity, we should expect to rub each other up the wrong way. You might think that celebrating Jesus and 'Peace on Earth' means arguing is less likely, but even Jesus' disciples argued – even when He was right there with them! One of their arguments reveals something of the strange wisdom of Christmas.

Brothers James and John had decided that they wanted to organise the seating arrangements for when Jesus came into His glory. They sound like toddlers at the Christmas dinner table, but seating themselves next to Jesus was actually a power play. It was a political move, vying for significance in Jesus' Cabinet. This aggravated the other disciples and soon there was major conflict in the ranks.

Jesus intervenes. He explains that in His kingdom, power is not a means to get what you want in life but a means to serve others. He turns every expectation of the world on its head and summarises the Christmas message in a handy sound bite: 'the Son of Man did not come to be served, but to serve, and to give his life as a ransom for many' (v45).

Why did Jesus come to Earth at Christmas? Was it an ego trip? Did He expect to be fawned over? Did He need waiting on hand and foot?

No, Jesus, the Servant King, put the needs of others ahead of His own, sacrificing His life for the sake of those in need.

When I visited the US Embassy in London, the dark-suited, short-haired, sturdy security officers stationed at every door were intimidating. Each had been trained to take a bullet for those they were protecting. The logic is simple: their lives are less important than their ambassador's, and so they stand in the line of fire if necessary to keep the dignitary safe. But Jesus, a dignitary par excellence, is prepared to take the bullet for those beneath Him. The King is born to die for His people.

In light of our Lord Jesus' courage and humility, the least we can do is to reconsider what we are likely to argue about this Christmas. When we are tempted to look down on others or put them down even slightly; when we are tempted to jostle for attention, praise or control; let us remember Jesus' Christmas challenge to serve, not be served.

Ponder

Think about the power politics in your workplace and family. Consider the contrast with Jesus' use of power.

Question to Consider

How can we help keep – or bring – the peace in our families this Christmas?

Closing Prayer

Lord Jesus, You are the King of kings – and yet You came to serve. Help me to graciously love and serve others, remembering all the while that in serving them, I am blessed to be able to serve You, my King. Amen.

DAY 28

Strange Life

Bible Reading

John 10:7–10

'Very truly I tell you, I am the gate for the sheep... I have come that they may have life, and have it to the full.' (vv7,10)

Daily Focus

One of the occupational hazards of watching television around Christmas time is the advertising. Take the plethora of perfume ads that appear this time of year for example – they make no sense at all. Chanel No. 5, one of the world's best-selling fragrances, may well have a floral bouquet with a hint of rose and jasmine but, bizarrely, you wouldn't know that from the ad. Instead, immaculately dressed celebrities pout, or drive fast cars, or walk through stunning landscapes surrounded by opulence and splendour. The perfume industry, now worth over £25 billion a year, offers not a smell, but a style. And customers are pulled in by the millions, in the hope of finding a better life – in a bottle.

Jesus explains that He came into the world to offer us a genuinely better life. But strangely, Jesus uses an unglamorous illustration to drive this point home. He refuses the flattery and elitism of the perfume industry, instead equating humans to smelly sheep and (radically) God to a smelly shepherd and Himself to a farm gate.

Jesus says that anyone promising a better life through any other means is like a thief, ultimately intending only to steal and destroy. They are like those perfume sellers. They promise the world, but really they just want to steal your money for themselves. The product may not make you happier, but it will definitely make someone else richer.

We learn to become cynical about the power of advertising. But why trust Jesus' Christmas message that He came to offer us a better life? Jesus, as designer of the heavens and earth, knows better than anyone what life in all its fullness really means. Jesus, who demonstrated His love to us by His birth, life and death, is not seeking to make a quick profit off us. His commitment to us gives great credibility. He does not promise to give us the luxurious life that advertisers are selling. Jesus' unglamourous illustration points to life lived with dirty hands, and a pure and loving heart.

I know the fallacious claims of the Christmas advertising. I know that buying that aftershave won't make me look like Johnny Depp. I know that cologne won't convert my car into a classic. I know that buying that scent for my wife won't transform dull, grey clouds into a breath-taking sunset. But I also know that choosing to follow the voice of the shepherd, and trusting Him for life in all its fullness – His promises will not fail me.

Ponder

The increasing commercialisation of Christmas puts the true and radical message of Christmas into ever greater contrast. The world wants a better life, and we are the ones to point to a different gateway.

Question to Consider

How does the life modelled by Jesus differ from the life that advertisers try to sell to us?

Closing Prayer

Lord Jesus, trusted shepherd, help me to hear Your voice alone and to follow You to abundant life. Amen.

DAY 29

Strange Charity

Bible Reading

Luke 4:18–19

'The Spirit of the Lord is on me, because he has anointed me to proclaim good news to the poor.' (v18)

Daily Focus

It is hard to go to a shopping centre at Christmas without someone asking you to give them your money. The homeless gather, recognising that shoppers playing fast and loose with their cash may be willing to part with a few more coins. The charity fundraisers shake their tins and wave their standing orders. Sometimes we are motivated to give by guilt. We feel bad about the excessive consumerism we are participating in and try to offset it with some token of kindness to others. Sometimes we give because deep down we know that Christmas has something to do with charity, compassion and generosity.

Jesus wanted people to understand the wisdom of Christmas, and so early in His ministry He went to the synagogue and read aloud from the scroll handed to Him. It is telling that on this particular Sabbath the pre-assigned Scripture reading began with Chapter 61 of Isaiah, which Jesus closed with the shocking words: 'Today this scripture is fulfilled' (v21).

This is Jesus' first official public engagement. Like the first speech of a Prime Minister on the steps of 10 Downing Street, or a new President addressing the nation from the White House Rose Garden, this is a defining moment. Jesus explains that He is the fulfilment of the time of God's favour. His mission is not for the mainstream or the most important, but for the poor and marginalised. It is a strange identification in a world that ignored the poor or even worse – blamed the poor for their circumstances. It is an identification that Jesus would live out; He spent most of His time with the poor, and freeing people from disease and death.

Isaiah's prophecy talks about proclaiming both the year of the Lord's favour and the day of God's vengeance. But Jesus stops midsentence. This is significant for Advent. The priority of Jesus' mission of coming into the world that first Christmas was to offer hope and grace to all who would accept it, particularly the poor and needy. But Jesus will come again, and this time it won't be to proclaim the Lord's favour, but instead to bring God's judgment.

As we celebrate the coming of Christ that first Christmas, and as we prepare for Jesus to come again, let us check we are following His priorities. Jesus' reason for coming into the world is defined by how He relates to the most vulnerable in society. Our relationship with poverty cannot be restricted to a few conscience-easing coins in a collection plate. We must be willing to follow Jesus as He blazes a trail for us towards demonstrating the grace of God to the poor and the oppressed everywhere.

Ponder

Just like serving Christmas dinner to the children first, so Jesus prioritises the poor. God loves all people, but He makes sure that the most vulnerable are at the front of the queue.

Question to Consider

Poverty and debt is a real problem for many people, often particularly felt at Christmas. How can we share the good news of a Saviour born to alleviate poverty?

Closing Prayer

Lord Jesus, You traded the riches of heaven for our hearts, and in place of our poverty You give us a place in Your kingdom. How can we thank You enough? Amen.

DAY 30

Strange Division

Bible Reading

Luke 12:49–53

'Do you think I came to bring peace on earth? No, I tell you, but division. From now on there will be five in one family divided against each other' (vv51–52)

Daily Focus

Father Christmas is a perfect symbol for a consumer society. He encourages us to show our love through buying gifts for people. So perhaps it is understandable that in every shopping centre and on every high street you visit this season, you are likely to hear more about him than about Jesus. The Father Christmas myth is loosely based on the story of St Nicholas, a Christian bishop from fourth-century Greece. St Nick was the original Father Christmas and he was famous for his generosity to the poor. He most famously provided the wedding dowries for the daughters of poor families so that they could get married and avoid falling into poverty and perhaps prostitution. Somehow we have taken this story of Christian charity and morphed it into a mascot to fit our commercial lifestyles.

But there is another dark side to the Father Christmas myth. Woe betide you if you fall off his nice list and onto his naughty list. It is strange that even in the secularised form of Christmas celebrations, there is a recognition of moral discernment, division and judgment.

Is there a dark side to Jesus too? Does He too judge between those who have been naughty and nice, dividing us into those worthy of reward or punishment?

Jesus is not easily co-opted into a capitalist branding campaign, because He has the annoying habit of calling for generosity to the needy, and not substituting money for love. And some of His teaching is uncomfortable, like the one where He says He is bringing division, fire and judgment. This seems more in line with Santa's naughty and nice list than the angel song promising 'Peace on Earth'.

Jesus was paradoxically both a great unifier and a great divider of people. He included those usually rejected by society. And He earned Himself many enemies in the process. Jesus' dividing line is not about who is naughty and nice – the Bible (and life in general) shows that we would all fail that test. The dividing line is between those who welcome Jesus' message, and those who refuse to welcome it. The dividing line is between those who welcome the vulnerable as Jesus did, and those who refuse to associate with the needy. Jesus knows this dividing line will cut through families. Ancestry and genetics will not guarantee a place in Jesus' family. Each individual must choose for themselves which side of the line to stand on.

And so we have a choice to make. Will we recognise our need of God's grace? Are we willing to share it with others?

Ponder

There are some family conflicts at Christmas that we can appease through an attitude of humility. However, when our families are divided in our response to Jesus at Christmas, then we can be encouraged that this is to be expected until Jesus comes again. In the meantime, we keep praying for them!

Question to Consider

Santa vs Jesus: where are the points of convergence and conflict?

Closing Prayer

Lord Jesus, You long to gather us together like a mother hen gathers her chicks. May we help our friends and family, strangers and enemies to choose a right response to You. Amen.

DAY 31

Strange Salvation

Bible Reading

1 Timothy 1:15–17

'Christ Jesus came into the world to save sinners – of whom I am the worst.' (v15)

Daily Focus

As a child, I once bought my mum an album by Lionel Richie. This was not a good Christmas present. First, it was a terrible album. Second, I bought it for her because I wanted it for myself. I am ashamed now of my short-sightedness and selfishness. I take some comfort, however, from the fact that I have received worse presents. One thoughtless person gave me the same gift I had bought them the previous year. Someone too stingy to buy me flowers once gave me a packet of seeds. Finding people who fail worse than me always makes me feel better about myself.

The apostle Paul does not have that self-protection reaction. He describes himself as the worst – and with good reason! He did hunt down and imprison Christians, stoning at least one to death. But I can think of worse people. What about Herod, the king who murdered countless babies and toddlers? What about those people who carried out the execution of Jesus Himself? Paul does not try to justify himself or measure himself up against the failings of others. He has been convicted of his sin and knows he has failed miserably.

Maybe you feel a failure. It doesn't make a difference when people tell you that it could have been worse. It doesn't help to think that you can offset it with doing good. You have failed and you know you cannot excuse it, deny it or ignore it.

This is when we need to hear the wisdom of Christmas that Paul takes comfort from: Jesus came into the world to save sinners. Jesus was not born in a stable in Bethlehem for those who feel good about themselves. He did not come to earth to rescue those who don't need rescuing, thank you very much. The promised Messiah came to save self-confessed sinners. He did so to show the world His great and strange patience and mercy.

We have seen the strangeness of God at work in this Christmas story. We have seen the strange wait that God made the world endure until just the right time for Jesus to be born. We have heard the strange worship songs that humans and angels sang in response to Christ's birth. We have experienced the strange welcome that God showed to the unlikeliest of people. And finally, we have looked at the strange wisdom of Christmas as we have sought to understand why Jesus was sent into the world. He came to save us and adopt us, to divide us and challenge us, to bring us fullness of life now and for ever.

Ponder

When the Salvation Army entered a new location, they would deliberately seek out the least likely convert. Through teaching and hospitality, they would help them trust Jesus, so everyone knew that God could save the worst of sinners.

Questions to Consider

When do you most feel a failure? How can you find comfort and hope in this passage?

Closing Prayer

Now to the King eternal, immortal, invisible, the only God, be honour and glory for ever and ever. Amen.

Group Study Notes

There are many ways to conduct a Bible study with others. Perhaps the most obvious is gathering together in person to talk and pray. This guide imagines you'll be able to do just that, once a week through the course of Advent.

If it's tough to find a time to get together, why not consider a group email discussion or another form of group chat (perhaps on WhatsApp, Skype or something similar)? Each person (or a leader) can post questions and thoughts that everyone can see and respond to. You might be able to work together daily on this basis, or as and when you can.

If you choose to gather in the traditional way, you may want to reflect back which of the daily focuses you found particularly challenging or helpful. You may wish to raise questions, or make some observations or connections of your own. Or you may prefer to discuss the session as a whole and consider and apply the theme for the week. There may be issues that are particularly poignant for someone in your group, and it could be good to share responses and pray together.

An open discussion can lead to some profound places without any need for guidance. But sometimes a little steering may help, and the following pages suggest some ways to guide and encourage discussion and do some further research. If the strangeness of Christmas has piqued your curiosity, you can learn more of the oddness of God in my latest book *God Is Stranger.**

I pray that my brief thoughts will be helpful. I pray that each member of your group will be encouraged and provoked in their faith, and grasp something deeper of the significance of the Christmas message this Advent.

*Krish Kandiah, *God Is Stranger: What happens when God turns up?* (London: Hodder & Stoughton, 2018)

SESSION ONE: STRANGE WAIT

Whether we are looking forward to or dreading something, waiting is a strange and difficult thing. We quickly get impatient, especially when there are problems around us that need fixing. Our studies in this session have noted the mess we often find ourselves in: challenges of our circumstances, families, spiritual lives, anxieties, sufferings, churches and homes. Let us take heart and learn from the generations of God's people who waited for the first Christmas.

Read

Psalm 37:1–40

Discuss

1. Imagine you are at the doctor's surgery and your ten-minute wait turns into a two-hour wait. What do you do?
2. What problems in your life are you waiting to see fixed?
3. What does waiting look like according to Psalm 37?
4. Why is the wait for the promised Messiah such a long, strange one? Why do you think God took so long in sending Jesus?
5. Which of the following statements is important for you?
   - Waiting helps me to reflect on God's plan
   - Waiting helps me to put things in perspective
   - Waiting helps me to learn patience
   - Waiting teaches me to trust God's promises
   - Waiting gives me time to prepare myself
   - Waiting gives the opportunity to see transformation
6. How can we help one another to wait expectantly for Jesus' coming?

Before praying to close, why not spend five minutes in silence to acknowledge that you are prepared to wait for God – in your life, and in the timing of His return.

SESSION TWO: STRANGE WORSHIP

Christmas is a very musical time of year. There are carols, pop classics, children's songs and television jingles that are recycled every December (if not earlier) to help get us into the festive mood. Some are better than others! This week we have looked at some of the original songs in the Christmas story and seen how they teach us things that are strange, but true. Each of them inspires us to worship God afresh this Christmas.

Read

Psalm 98:1–9

Discuss

1. What is your all-time favourite Christmas song and why?
2. Why do you think the Bible records so many songs as part of the Christmas story?
3. Mary and Joseph, angels and shepherds, Elizabeth and Zechariah, Anna and Simeon, Old Testament prophets and New Testament apostles: each has a unique song to sing. Which do you most closely relate to?
4. If you were to write your own Christmas song, what would your inspiration be (eg snow, presents, food, Jesus)?
5. Apart from singing, what other ways can you think of to worship God?
6. Meditate on Psalm 98, the inspiration behind Isaac Watts' carol *Joy to the World*. How does it help us in understanding why we should worship God, how we should worship Him, and who should worship Him?

Perhaps finish your session today listening to a Christmas song that helps you focus on the real meaning of the Advent season.

SESSION THREE: STRANGE WELCOME

At the heart of the Christmas story is the theme of welcome and hospitality. Will the world have room for the Christ-child? Mary and Joseph make room, but they find no room available to them in Bethlehem. Mary makes room for shepherds and travellers, who arrive to welcome Jesus. Herod has no room for Jesus, even as a baby. And by the time Jesus is grown up, the world has no room for Him either. He dies on the cross so that God can make room for us in His family. Jesus leaves us with a challenge – those who welcome His children will be welcomed into heaven.

Read

Matthew 18:1–14

Discuss

1. Unusual guests always make for memorable Christmases. Share your stories of unexpected people around your Christmas table.
2. What does it mean to you that you are welcomed into God's family?
3. How many ways does Matthew underline God's particular care for children in the above verses?
4. Think of ways in which you, your family and your church could make room for children this Christmas.
5. Think of ways in which you, your family and your church could welcome outsiders this Christmas.
6. 'Welcoming Jesus, welcoming strangers is to welcome suffering too.' Why is this true? Why does God ask us to do this anyway?

Finish by reflecting on the fact that we offer hospitality not because we are told to, but because God first offered the greatest hospitality to us: He gave us His world to live in, His purpose to share in, and His family to be a part of.

SESSION FOUR: STRANGE WISDOM

Why was Jesus born as a baby in Bethlehem two millennia ago? This week we've looked at God's strange wisdom in this. Jesus was born to die, to save us, to adopt us into His family, to give us life in all its fullness, and perhaps also to bring division. How is a newborn baby sleeping on straw going to fulfil all of this? To grasp something of God's strange plan is to help us understand the significance of celebrating Christmas.

Read

1 Corinthians 1:26–31

Discuss

1. Why does your family celebrate Christmas?
2. How many reasons can you think of for God sending Jesus into the world? Which reason is most significant to you right now? How is it reflected in your celebrations?
3. Which of those reasons do you struggle most to grasp? How can you grow in understanding this Christmas?
4. How does the passage above help you to understand God's decision to send Jesus as a baby?
5. 'God chose the weak things of the world to shame the strong' (v27). What encouragement can you receive from this verse?
6. From the entire series, what encouragements can you offer to one another as a Christmas blessing?

Here is my Christmas blessing for all of you:

Keep on loving one another as brothers and sisters. Do not forget to show hospitality to strangers, for by so doing some people have shown hospitality to angels without knowing it (Heb. 13:1–2). Amen.

So much of Christmas is about welcome. As an adult, Jesus said, 'whoever welcomes a child in my name, welcomes me'. Today, there are thousands of vulnerable children who need a welcome – a bed for a night, a refuge for a while, a home for good.

Home for Good exists to find a home for every child who needs one. We want all children and young people in care to thrive in a safe and loving family environment, whether through foster care or adoption.

We raise awareness in the Church of the needs of vulnerable children, inspiring families to consider fostering or adoption and equipping churches to be safe and welcoming for all children and young people and to offer wrap-around support to families. We produce resources, provide training, and we campaign to create better outcomes for vulnerable children and the families who care for them. Everything we do helps to improve the well-being of children in care, both today and in the years to come.

Could you welcome a child who needs a home for good?

Get in touch to find out more about Home for Good, fostering or adoption.

homeforgood.org.uk
0300 001 0995
info@homeforgood.org.uk
176 Copenhagen Street, London, N1 0ST

Cover to Cover Bible Studies for Lent

Ideal for group or individual use

NEW TITLE

Who is The Christ?

by Anne Calver

Anne Calver invites us to take a look at six different aspects of Christ's character, so that we might dwell on who He really is and the marks that He left on the world. Through six studies, discover fresh insights into the person of Jesus, and how He revealed the nature of God.

ISBN: 978-1-78259-760-5

Living Faith: Invitations from the cross

by Krish Kandiah

Krish Kandiah brings his Bible knowledge and contemporary edge to this Lent Bible study guide. Explore the seven sayings of the cross and discover how these are a personal invitation from God, encouraging us to connect with Him on a deeper level.

ISBN: 978-1-78259-691-2

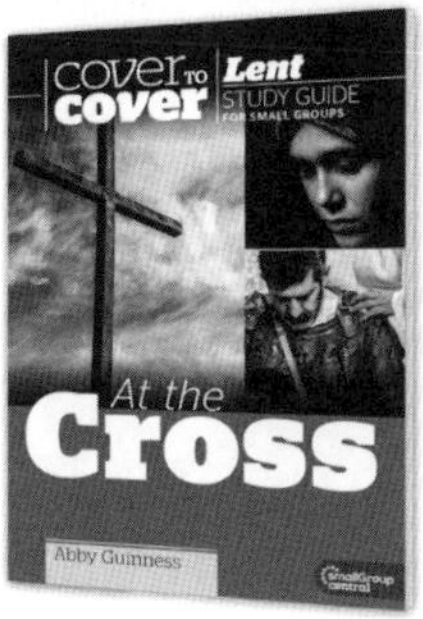

At the Cross

by Abby Guinness

Approach the cross from a new direction during Lent by considering the perspectives of those present at Christ's crucifixion. Each of the six sessions includes Bible readings and fictional eyewitness monologues with textual and historical insights.

ISBN: 978-1-78259-498-7

To find out about all our Lent titles, for current prices and to order, visit **cwr.org.org.uk/shop**
Available online or from Christian bookshops.

SmallGroup central

All of our small group ideas and resources in one place

Online:

www.smallgroupcentral.org.uk is filled with free video teaching, tools, articles and a whole host of ideas.

On the road:

A range of seminars themed for small groups can be brought to your local community. Contact us at ***hello@smallgroupcentral.org.uk***

In print:

Books, study guides and DVDs covering an extensive list of themes, Bible books and life issues.

Find out more at:
www.smallgroupcentral.org.uk

TRANSFORMED LIVING

TRANSFORMED LIFE

cover to cover

Every Day with Jesus extra

40 JESUS

Liz Babbs STUDY GUIDE

Life JOURNEYS

vital:

Small Group ToolBox